TODAY'S GREAT QUARTERBACKS

TOM BRADY

By Ryan Nagelhout

Gareth Stevens
Publishing

RIGHT ON!

Please visit our website www.garethstevens.com. For a free color catalog of all our high-quality books, call toll free 1-800-542-2595 or fax 1-877-542-2596.

Library of Congress Cataloging-in-Publication Data

Nagelhout, Ryan.
Tom Brady / by Ryan Nagelhout.
 p. cm. — (Today's great quarterbacks)
Includes index.
ISBN 978-1-4824-0150-9 (pbk.)
ISBN 978-1-4824-0151-6 (6-pack)
ISBN 978-1-4824-0148-6 (library binding)
1. Brady, Tom, — 1977- — Juvenile literature. 2. Football players — United States — Biography — Juvenile literature. I. Nagelhout, Ryan. II. Title.
GV939.B685 N34 2014
796.332092—dc23

First Edition

Published in 2014 by
Gareth Stevens Publishing
111 East 14th Street, Suite 349
New York, NY 10003

Copyright © 2014 Gareth Stevens Publishing

Designer: Nicholas Domiano
Editor: Ryan Nagelhout

Photo credits: Cover, p. 1 Jared Wickerham/Getty Images Sport/Getty Images; p. 5 Jerritt Clark/FilmMagic/Getty Images; p. 7 Jim Rogash/Getty Images Sport/Getty Images; p. 9 Gregory Shamus/Getty Image Sport/Getty Images; p. 11 KMazur/WireImage/Getty Images; p. 13 Rick Stewart/Hulton Archive/Getty Images; p. 15 Jamie Squire/Hulton Archive/Getty Images; p. 17 Jed Jacobsohn/Getty Images Sport/Getty Images; pp. 19, 23 Elsa/Getty Images Sport/Getty Images; p. 21 Tom Szczerbowski/Getty Images Sport/Getty Images; p. 25 Jamie McCarthy/WireImage/Getty Images; p. 27 Joe Kohen/Getty Images Entertainment/Getty Images; p. 29 Donna Connor/WireImage/Getty Images.

Printed in the United States of America

CPSIA compliance information: Batch #CW14GS: For further information contact Gareth Stevens, New York, New York at 1-800-542-2595.

CONTENTS

Meet Tom

Tom Brady is a champion quarterback. He plays in the **National Football League** (NFL).

Thomas Edward Patrick Brady was born on August 3, 1977, in San Mateo, California. His parents are named Galynn and Thomas.

Tom went to Junipero Serra High School in San Mateo. He played quarterback there for two seasons. He also played baseball.

Catching, Not Throwing

Tom was a catcher in high school. In 1995, he was picked by the Montreal Expos in the 18th round of the Major League Baseball **Draft**.

Tom went to the University of Michigan to play **college** football in 1996. He started at quarterback for parts of his junior and senior years.

Tom was picked by the New England Patriots 199th overall in the 2000 NFL Draft. Professional teams didn't expect much from him.

Super Patriots

Tom started at quarterback early in the 2001 season. He led the Patriots all the way to a win in Super Bowl 36! He was named the game's Most Valuable Player (MVP).

In 2004, the Patriots beat the Carolina Panthers in Super Bowl 38. Tom was named the game's MVP. The Patriots also won Super Bowl 39 in 2005.

Record Setter

Tom won the NFL MVP award in 2007. He set the NFL record for touchdowns in a season. Tom played in his fourth Super Bowl that season.

Tom missed most of the 2008 season with a knee injury. In 2009, Tom won the league's **Comeback** Player of the Year award.

Family Man

Tom married model Gisele Bündchen in 2009. They have two kids, Benjamin and Vivian.

Tom loves to help **charities**. He works with Best Buddies International and the Boys and Girls Club of America in Massachusetts.

Super Again

Tom Brady and the Patriots made another Super Bowl appearance in 2011. In 2015, they won again! Brady won his third MVP award, too!

29

Timeline

1977   Thomas Edward Patrick Brady is born on August 3.

1996   Tom attends the University of Michigan to play football.

2000   The Patriots pick Tom 199th overall in the NFL Draft.

2002   Tom leads the Patriots to win in Super Bowl 36. Tom is named MVP.

2004   The Patriots win Super Bowl 38. Tom is named MVP.

2007   Tom sets NFL record for touchdowns thrown in a season.

2009   Tom marries Gisele Bündchen.

2015   Patriots win Super Bowl 49. Tom wins third MVP award.

For More Information

Books

Allen, Kathy. *Tom Brady*. New York, NY: Bearport Publishing, 2013.

Gitlin, Marty. *Tom Brady: Super Bowl Quarterback*. Minneapolis, MN: ABDO Publishing, 2012.

Websites

Tom Brady's Official Fan Page

facebook.com/TomBrady

Visit Tom Brady's official Facebook page and stay up to date with the NFL superstar.

Tom Brady's Stats Page

patriots.com/team/roster/Tom-Brady/272d4f2c-1bb9-4372-b02c-dfa3fa60575b

Find statistics, photos, video, and more on the official Patriots team site.

Publisher's note to educators and parents: Our editors have carefully reviewed these websites to ensure that they are suitable for students. Many websites change frequently, however, and we cannot guarantee that a site's future contents will continue to meet our high standards of quality and educational value. Be advised that students should be closely supervised whenever they access the Internet.

Glossary

charity: giving aid to people in need

college: a school after high school

comeback: a return to a former condition

draft: to pick something, a way for sports teams to pick new players

National Football League: the top football league in the United States

Index